KNOWSLEY LIBRARY SERVICE

Knowsl@y Council

Please return this book on or before the date shown below

PROJECT LOAN

How Plants Grow

Claire Llewellyn

W
FRANKLIN WATTS
LONDON • SYDNEY

First published in 2005 by Franklin Watts
96 Leonard Street, London EC2A 4XD

Franklin Watts Australia
Level 17/207 Kent Street, Sydney NSW 2000

Text copyright © Claire Llewellyn 2005
Design and concept © Franklin Watts 2005

Series adviser: Gill Matthews, non-fiction literacy
    consultant and Inset trainer
Series editor: Rachel Cooke
Editor: Sarah Ridley
Series design: Peter Scoulding
Designer: Jemima Lumley
Acknowledgements: Frank Blackburn/Ecoscene 12; Laurie Campbell/NHPA 5t, 7;
Chris Fairclough cover, 13br; Franklin Watts Library 20, 21b; thanks to Gossypium 21tr; Chinch
Gryniewicz/Ecoscene 6, 22l; T Kitchin and V Hurst/NHPA 15; Ray Moller imprint page, 9tr, 10, 11,
14, 15r, 15b, 22r, 23l; Sally Morgan/Ecoscene 4, 5b; Christophe Ratier/NHPA 13l; Steve Shott title
page, 16, 17, 18, 19, 23r; Barrie Watts 8, 9l, 15b.

A CIP catalogue record for this book is available from the British Library.

ISBN: 0 7496 6362 6

Dewey decimal classification number: 571.8'2

Printed in Malaysia

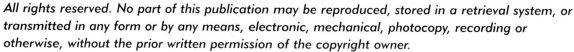

Contents

All kinds of plants

There are many different plants. They come in all shapes and sizes.

▶ *This redwood tree is very tall.*

How are these plants different from one another? How are they the same?

▲ *These daisies are small.*

▶ *This cactus is spiky.*

All kinds of places

Plants grow all over the world. The place a plant grows is called its habitat.

▶ *Waterlilies grow in rivers and ponds.*

▼ *Pine trees grow on mountains.*

Look around your school grounds. Which plants grow there?

A seed grows

Most plants grow from seeds. When a seed is warm and damp, it begins to sprout.

Shoot

▼ **Day 1** *A bean seed is planted.*

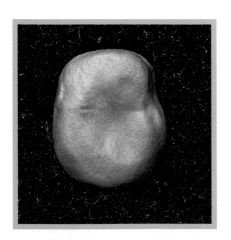

▶ **Day 7** *The seed grows a root and a shoot.*

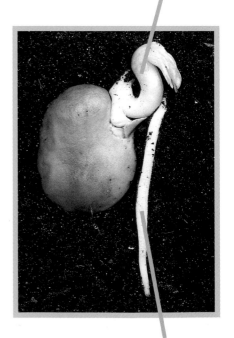

Root

▶ **Day 21** *The plant is growing bigger. It has leaves and a stem now.*

Grow some broad bean seeds in a jam jar with damp cotton wool.

Leaf

Stem

Root

9

The parts of a plant

Most plants have the same parts. They have roots, a stem and leaves. Many plants also have flowers.

Flower

Leaf

Stem

Roots

◀ *The stem of a tree is called its trunk.*

Collect three different leaves and draw them.

▶ *Leaves are different shapes and colours.*

Flowers and seeds

Most plants grow flowers. The flowers make seeds for the plants inside the fruit.

Petal

Fruit

▶ *The fruit forms at the centre of the poppy flower. Inside it are the seeds.*

The poppy's petals have fallen off. Tiny black seeds are spilling out of the fruit.

Many flowers have bright colours and a sweet smell. Which is your favourite flower?

13

Fruit and seeds

Many plants make their seeds inside a fruit.

▲ *All these fruits have seeds inside them.*

This apple tree is heavy with ripe fruit. There are seeds inside the apples.

A tomato is a kind of fruit. It has lots of seeds.

Plants need light

Plants need light to grow.
Without light, they will slowly die.

◀ *This cress has been left to grow in the light for a week.*

This cress has been left to grow in the dark for a week.

What do you notice about the cress?

Plants need water

Plants need water to grow. Their roots suck it up from the ground.

▶ *This plant looks healthy. Its soil is damp.*

18

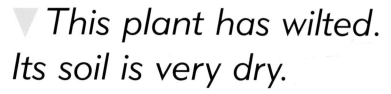 *This plant has wilted. Its soil is very dry.*

How quickly do roots suck up water? Put a dry pot plant in a saucer of water. Time how long it takes for the water to disappear.

Useful plants

Many plants give us useful things.

▼ *Plants give us food. We eat some of the fruits, seeds and other parts of the plant.*

▶ We make clothes from the fibres of the cotton plant.

▼ Trees give us wood. We make many things from wood.

Look around you. How many things can you see that are made from plants?

I know that...

1 There are many different kinds of plants.

2 Plants grow in all sorts of places.

3 Most plants grow from seeds.

4 Plants have roots, a stem and leaves.

5 A plant's flowers make seeds.

6 Seeds are often found inside fruit.

7 Plants need light to grow.

8 They need water, too.

9 Plants give us food and other useful things.

Index

About this book

I Know That! is designed to introduce children to the process of gathering information and using reference books, one of the key skills needed to begin more formal learning at school. For this reason, each book's structure reflects the information books children will use later in their learning career – with key information in the main text and additional facts and ideas in the captions. The panels give an opportunity for further activities, ideas or discussions. The contents page and index are helpful reference guides.

The language is carefully chosen to be accessible to children just beginning to read. Illustrations support the text but also give information in their own right; active consideration and discussion of images is another key referencing skill. The main aim of the series is to build confidence – showing children how much they already know and giving them the ability to gather new information for themselves. With this in mind, the *I know that...* section at the end of the book is a simple way for children to revisit what they already know as well as what they have learnt from reading the book.